EMMANUEL JOSEPH

The Anatomy of Myth, How Ancient Stories Shape Modern Healing and Design

Copyright © 2025 by Emmanuel Joseph

All rights reserved. No part of this publication may be reproduced, stored or transmitted in any form or by any means, electronic, mechanical, photocopying, recording, scanning, or otherwise without written permission from the publisher. It is illegal to copy this book, post it to a website, or distribute it by any other means without permission.

First edition

This book was professionally typeset on Reedsy.
Find out more at reedsy.com

Contents

1	Chapter 1: The Origins of Myth	1
2	Chapter 2: The Psychological Impact of Myths	3
3	Chapter 3: Myths and Healing Practices	5
4	Chapter 4: Mythical Archetypes in Design	7
5	Chapter 5: The Symbolism of Mythological Creatures	9
6	Chapter 6: Myth and Architecture	11
7	Chapter 7: The Mythic Roots of Storytelling	13
8	Chapter 8: Myth in Visual Arts	15
9	Chapter 9: The Role of Myth in Cultural Identity	17
10	Chapter 10: Myth and Modern Technology	19
11	Chapter 11: The Future of Myth	21
12	Chapter 12: Conclusion	22
13	Chapter 13: Myth in Popular Culture	23
14	Chapter 14: The Intersection of Myth and Science	24
15	Chapter 15: Myth and Personal Transformation	25

1

Chapter 1: The Origins of Myth

The roots of mythology can be traced back to the earliest human civilizations. These stories were not merely tales told for entertainment; they were vital tools for making sense of the world. Myths provided explanations for natural phenomena, human behavior, and societal structures. The ancient Greeks, for instance, used their pantheon of gods to explain everything from the changing seasons to the complexities of human emotions. Similarly, the myths of ancient Egypt were intertwined with their understanding of life, death, and the cosmos.

These stories were passed down orally, evolving with each retelling. As societies grew more complex, so too did their myths. The transition from oral to written traditions allowed for the preservation of these stories, ensuring their survival through the ages. This chapter delves into the origins of myth, exploring how early humans crafted these narratives and the roles they played in their societies.

Mythology served not only as a means of explaining the unknown but also as a way to establish and maintain social order. Through myths, societies conveyed their values, norms, and beliefs. These narratives reinforced the idea of a shared history and identity, fostering a sense of unity and belonging among community members. As a result, myths became an essential part of cultural heritage, passed down through generations as a way to preserve and transmit collective knowledge.

The influence of myths extended beyond their immediate cultural context, as they often traveled across borders and were adapted by different societies. This cross-cultural exchange enriched the mythological tapestry, resulting in a diverse and interconnected web of stories. For example, the Greek myth of Hercules shares similarities with the Sumerian epic of Gilgamesh, highlighting the universality of certain themes and archetypes. This chapter will explore how myths evolved and spread, shaping the cultural landscapes of various civilizations.

Finally, the chapter will examine the role of myths in shaping human understanding and perception. By providing a framework for interpreting the world, myths influenced the way people thought, acted, and related to one another. The enduring power of these ancient stories lies in their ability to resonate with the fundamental aspects of the human experience, transcending time and cultural boundaries. As we delve into the origins of myth, we uncover the timeless wisdom embedded within these narratives, offering valuable insights into the human condition.

2

Chapter 2: The Psychological Impact of Myths

Myths are more than just stories; they are reflections of the human psyche. Carl Jung, a prominent psychologist, proposed that myths are manifestations of the collective unconscious, a concept that encompasses the shared experiences and archetypes common to all humans. These archetypes, such as the hero, the mother, and the trickster, are deeply ingrained in our psyches and continue to influence our thoughts, behaviors, and dreams.

Modern psychology has embraced the therapeutic potential of myths. Techniques such as Jungian analysis and mythotherapy use these ancient stories to help individuals uncover and address deep-seated psychological issues. By engaging with myths, patients can gain insights into their own lives, drawing parallels between their personal experiences and the universal themes found in these tales. This chapter examines the profound psychological impact of myths and their therapeutic applications.

Myths also serve as a mirror, reflecting the societal norms and values of the times in which they were created. By analyzing these stories, psychologists and historians can gain a deeper understanding of the collective consciousness of past civilizations. For instance, the prominence of hero myths in various cultures suggests a universal human desire for strength, resilience, and the triumph over adversity. This chapter will explore how these psychological insights are derived from mythological narratives.

Furthermore, myths can provide a sense of continuity and stability in an ever-changing world. They offer a framework for understanding the human experience, connecting individuals to their cultural heritage and the broader human story. In times of crisis or uncertainty, myths can serve as a source of comfort and guidance, reminding us of the timeless truths and values that have shaped human civilization. This chapter delves into the ways in which myths provide psychological support and foster a sense of connection and belonging.

3

Chapter 3: Myths and Healing Practices

Across cultures, myths have been intertwined with healing practices. Shamans, priests, and healers have long used mythological narratives to facilitate physical and spiritual healing. These stories often involve journeys to the underworld, encounters with divine beings, and trials of endurance, all of which symbolize the transformative process of healing.

In modern medicine, the influence of myth persists. Narrative medicine, an approach that emphasizes the importance of storytelling in the healing process, draws on the power of myths to help patients make sense of their illnesses and find meaning in their suffering. By integrating mythological elements into their narratives, patients can embark on their own heroic journeys toward recovery. This chapter explores the role of myths in traditional and contemporary healing practices.

Mythological stories often contain symbols and metaphors that resonate with the subconscious mind, facilitating emotional and psychological healing. For example, the motif of the hero's journey, with its trials and ultimate triumph, can inspire individuals to overcome their own challenges and embrace personal growth. This chapter will examine specific myths and their therapeutic applications, highlighting the ways in which these ancient narratives continue to promote healing and well-being.

In addition to their psychological benefits, myths can also influence physical healing. Studies have shown that the mind-body connection plays a crucial role in the healing process, and positive narratives can enhance the body's ability to recover from illness or injury. By drawing on the symbolism and themes of myths, healers can create powerful narratives that support both mental and physical healing. This chapter delves into the intersection of mythology and medicine, exploring the ways in which these ancient stories continue to shape modern healing practices.

4

Chapter 4: Mythical Archetypes in Design

The influence of myth extends beyond psychology and healing to the realm of design. Mythical archetypes, with their universal appeal and symbolic resonance, have long inspired architects, artists, and designers. These archetypes serve as powerful tools for creating spaces and objects that evoke specific emotions and responses.

For instance, the hero's journey, a common mythological motif, can be seen in the design of buildings and spaces that guide users through a transformative experience. The labyrinth, another archetypal symbol, has been used in garden design and architecture to create spaces for reflection and self-discovery. This chapter delves into the ways in which mythical archetypes shape modern design, from architecture to product design.

Designers often draw on mythological themes to create visually striking and emotionally resonant works. For example, the use of celestial motifs in interior design can evoke a sense of wonder and connection to the cosmos, while motifs inspired by nature can create a sense of harmony and balance. This chapter will explore the various ways in which mythological archetypes are incorporated into design, highlighting their ability to create meaningful and impactful spaces.

Furthermore, myths can inspire innovative design solutions that address contemporary challenges. By drawing on the timeless wisdom and symbolism of ancient stories, designers can create works that are not only aesthetically pleasing but also functional and sustainable. This chapter will examine case studies of myth-inspired design, showcasing the ways in which these ancient narratives continue to shape the creative process.

5

Chapter 5: The Symbolism of Mythological Creatures

Mythological creatures, from dragons to phoenixes, are rich in symbolic meaning. These fantastical beings often represent human fears, desires, and aspirations. In ancient myths, they were used to convey moral lessons, embody natural forces, and personify abstract concepts.

Modern designers continue to draw inspiration from these creatures, using their symbolism to create compelling visual narratives. For example, the dragon, a symbol of power and protection, is often incorporated into designs to evoke a sense of strength and majesty. Similarly, the phoenix, representing rebirth and renewal, is used to symbolize transformation and resilience. This chapter explores the symbolic significance of mythological creatures and their influence on contemporary design.

The symbolic meanings of mythological creatures can vary across cultures, reflecting the unique beliefs and values of different societies. For instance, while dragons are often seen as malevolent creatures in Western mythology, they are revered as benevolent and powerful beings in Eastern traditions. This chapter will explore the cultural variations in the symbolism of mythological creatures, highlighting their diverse and multifaceted nature.

In addition to their symbolic meanings, mythological creatures can also serve as powerful storytelling tools. By incorporating these fantastical beings into their designs, artists and designers can create narratives that captivate and inspire audiences. This chapter will examine specific examples of mythological creatures in contemporary design, showcasing the ways in which these ancient symbols continue to resonate in modern creative works.

6

Chapter 6: Myth and Architecture

Architecture has always been a medium through which myths are expressed. Ancient temples, pyramids, and monuments were often designed to embody the cosmological beliefs and mythological narratives of their creators. These structures served not only as places of worship but also as tangible representations of the myths that shaped their societies.

Today, architects continue to draw on mythological themes to create buildings that resonate with deeper meanings. The use of symbolic forms, motifs, and spatial arrangements can evoke mythic narratives, creating spaces that engage and inspire. This chapter examines the interplay between myth and architecture, exploring how ancient stories inform the design of modern buildings.

Myth-inspired architecture often incorporates elements that symbolize the journey of the human spirit. For example, the use of spiral staircases can represent the ascent to higher knowledge or spiritual enlightenment. Similarly, the incorporation of natural elements, such as water features and gardens, can evoke the harmony between humanity and nature found in many mythological narratives. This chapter delves into the specific design elements that draw on mythological themes, highlighting their impact on the built environment.

Furthermore, the chapter explores how mythological themes can be adapted to contemporary architectural challenges. By drawing on the timeless wisdom of ancient stories, architects can create buildings that are not only aesthetically pleasing but also functional and sustainable. This chapter showcases examples of modern architecture that successfully integrate mythological themes, demonstrating the enduring relevance of these ancient narratives in shaping the spaces we inhabit.

Chapter 7: The Mythic Roots of Storytelling

Storytelling is a fundamental human activity, and myths are among the earliest and most enduring forms of narrative. These stories, with their complex characters and intricate plots, have provided a template for countless works of literature, theater, and film.

The mythic structure, with its emphasis on the hero's journey, has become a cornerstone of modern storytelling. This chapter explores the evolution of storytelling from ancient myths to contemporary narratives, highlighting the enduring influence of these ancient tales on the art of storytelling.

Myths often follow a common structure, known as the monomyth or hero's journey, which involves a hero embarking on an adventure, facing trials, achieving a significant victory, and returning home transformed. This narrative framework has been used in countless stories across different cultures and time periods, from ancient epics like the "Odyssey" to modern blockbusters like "Star Wars." This chapter delves into the elements of the hero's journey and its significance in shaping storytelling traditions.

In addition to the hero's journey, myths also explore a wide range of themes and archetypes that resonate with the human experience. From the trickster figure who challenges societal norms to the wise old mentor who guides the hero, these archetypes continue to appear in contemporary stories, reflecting the timeless nature of these narratives. This chapter examines the various mythological themes and archetypes that have influenced storytelling across different mediums, demonstrating their ongoing relevance in modern culture.

8

Chapter 8: Myth in Visual Arts

The visual arts have long been a medium through which myths are brought to life. From ancient cave paintings to Renaissance masterpieces, artists have used their skills to depict mythological scenes and characters.

In contemporary art, the influence of myth remains strong. Artists continue to draw on mythological themes to explore complex ideas and emotions. This chapter examines the ways in which myths have been represented in visual arts throughout history and their ongoing impact on modern artistic expression.

Mythological themes can provide artists with a rich source of inspiration, allowing them to explore the deeper aspects of the human experience. For instance, the story of Icarus, who flew too close to the sun, has been depicted in various artworks to symbolize the consequences of hubris and the pursuit of ambition. Similarly, the myth of Narcissus, who fell in love with his own reflection, has been used to explore themes of vanity and self-obsession. This chapter delves into specific mythological stories and their visual representations, highlighting the ways in which artists use these narratives to convey complex ideas.

Moreover, the chapter explores how contemporary artists reinterpret and reimagine mythological themes to address current societal issues. By drawing on ancient stories, artists can create works that resonate with modern audiences, offering new perspectives on timeless themes. This chapter showcases examples of contemporary art that successfully integrate mythological elements, demonstrating the enduring power of these ancient narratives in shaping artistic expression.

9

Chapter 9: The Role of Myth in Cultural Identity

Myths play a crucial role in shaping cultural identity. They provide a sense of continuity, connecting the present with the past, and fostering a shared sense of heritage and belonging. In many cultures, myths are celebrated through rituals, festivals, and art forms, reinforcing their significance in contemporary society.

This chapter explores the role of myth in the formation of cultural identity, examining how these ancient stories continue to shape the values, beliefs, and traditions of modern communities.

Myths often serve as a source of national pride, highlighting the unique history and identity of a particular culture. For example, the myth of Romulus and Remus, the legendary founders of Rome, has been a central part of Roman identity for centuries. Similarly, the story of the Hindu god Rama and his epic journey in the "Ramayana" remains a significant cultural touchstone for millions of people in India and beyond. This chapter delves into specific myths and their roles in shaping cultural identities, highlighting their enduring relevance in contemporary society.

In addition to their role in cultural identity, myths can also promote cross-cultural understanding and dialogue. By exploring the common themes and archetypes found in different mythological traditions, individuals can gain a deeper appreciation for the shared human experience. This chapter examines the ways in which myths foster cultural exchange and understanding, showcasing their potential to bridge cultural divides and promote a sense of global unity.

10

Chapter 10: Myth and Modern Technology

The rapid advancement of technology has given rise to new forms of myth-making. The digital age has seen the emergence of new mythologies, from the cautionary tales of artificial intelligence and virtual reality to the utopian visions of space exploration and technological singularity.

These modern myths reflect our hopes, fears, and aspirations in the face of technological change. This chapter delves into the intersection of myth and technology, exploring how ancient narratives inform our understanding of the digital age.

The myths surrounding technology often draw on age-old themes and archetypes. For instance, the story of Prometheus, who stole fire from the gods to give to humanity, can be seen as a precursor to modern narratives about the power and potential dangers of technological innovation. Similarly, the tale of Icarus, who flew too close to the sun, serves as a cautionary reminder of the consequences of hubris and overreach. This chapter examines how these ancient myths continue to resonate in contemporary discussions about technology and its impact on society.

Furthermore, technology has also enabled new forms of storytelling, allowing myths to be reimagined and experienced in innovative ways. Virtual reality, augmented reality, and interactive digital media have opened up new possibilities for engaging with mythological narratives, creating immersive experiences that bring these ancient stories to life. This chapter explores the ways in which technology is transforming the way we interact with and understand myths, highlighting the enduring relevance of these narratives in the digital age.

11

Chapter 11: The Future of Myth

As we move into the future, the role of myth continues to evolve. While ancient myths provide a foundation for understanding the world, new myths are being created to address the challenges and opportunities of the modern age.

This chapter explores the future of myth, examining how these stories will continue to shape our lives and our world. From the enduring relevance of ancient tales to the creation of new narratives, myth remains a vital force in human culture.

The creation of new myths is an ongoing process, driven by the collective imagination of humanity. In an increasingly interconnected world, these stories often draw on diverse cultural traditions, blending elements from different mythological systems to create hybrid narratives that resonate with a global audience. This chapter delves into the emergence of new myths, exploring the ways in which they reflect contemporary concerns and aspirations.

Moreover, the chapter examines the potential for myths to inspire positive change and foster a sense of global unity. By drawing on the universal themes and archetypes found in mythological narratives, we can create stories that promote empathy, understanding, and cooperation across cultural boundaries. This chapter highlights the transformative power of myth and its potential to shape a better future for humanity.

12

Chapter 12: Conclusion

In "The Anatomy of Myth: How Ancient Stories Shape Modern Healing and Design," we have explored the enduring influence of myth on various aspects of contemporary life. From psychology and healing to design and architecture, these ancient stories continue to shape our understanding of the world and ourselves.

By examining the timeless wisdom embedded in these tales, we can gain new insights into the human experience and harness the power of myth to inspire creativity, foster healing, and design a better future. As we continue to navigate the complexities of the modern world, the lessons of myth remain as relevant and valuable as ever.

This journey through the anatomy of myth has revealed the profound ways in which these ancient stories continue to influence our lives. Whether through their psychological impact, their role in healing practices, or their inspiration for design and architecture, myths are an essential part of our cultural heritage. As we move forward, let us continue to draw on the wisdom of these timeless narratives, using them to guide us toward a more enlightened and harmonious future.

13

Chapter 13: Myth in Popular Culture

Myths have found a new home in popular culture, where they continue to captivate and inspire. From blockbuster movies and television shows to video games and comic books, mythological themes and characters have become a staple of modern entertainment. These stories resonate with audiences because they tap into universal themes and archetypes that are deeply ingrained in the human psyche.

This chapter explores the ways in which myths are represented in popular culture, highlighting their enduring appeal and cultural significance. By examining the ways in which these ancient stories are reimagined and adapted, we can gain a deeper understanding of the timeless nature of myth and its ability to evolve with the times.

Furthermore, the chapter delves into the impact of popular culture on our perception of myths. The widespread dissemination of mythological themes through various media has the potential to shape our collective consciousness and influence the way we understand and relate to these stories. This chapter showcases examples of myth in popular culture, demonstrating the ongoing relevance of these ancient narratives in contemporary society.

14

Chapter 14: The Intersection of Myth and Science

While myth and science are often seen as opposing forces, they share a common goal: to explain the world and our place in it. Throughout history, myths have provided explanations for natural phenomena and the mysteries of the universe. With the advent of modern science, many of these myths have been replaced by empirical knowledge, yet the influence of myth persists.

This chapter explores the intersection of myth and science, examining how ancient stories continue to inform and inspire scientific inquiry. By drawing on the symbolic and metaphorical language of myth, scientists and researchers can communicate complex ideas and concepts in a way that is accessible and engaging. This chapter delves into the ways in which myth and science complement each other, highlighting their shared quest for understanding.

Moreover, the chapter examines the role of myth in shaping scientific imagination and creativity. Many scientific discoveries and innovations have been inspired by mythological themes and narratives, demonstrating the enduring power of these ancient stories to spark curiosity and drive exploration. This chapter showcases examples of the interplay between myth and science, highlighting their mutual influence on human knowledge and progress.

15

Chapter 15: Myth and Personal Transformation

Myths have long been used as tools for personal growth and transformation. These stories often feature characters who undergo significant journeys, facing trials and challenges that lead to profound inner change. By engaging with these narratives, individuals can gain insights into their own lives and embark on their own journeys of self-discovery.

This chapter explores the role of myth in personal transformation, examining how these ancient stories can guide and inspire individuals on their paths to self-realization. By drawing on the symbolism and themes of myths, individuals can navigate the complexities of their inner worlds and embrace the transformative power of storytelling.

Book Description:

From the dawn of human civilization, myths have served as the foundation upon which societies build their understanding of the world. These ancient stories, with their rich tapestries of gods, heroes, and mythical creatures, have transcended time and space to continue influencing contemporary thought. In "The Anatomy of Myth: How Ancient Stories Shape Modern Healing and Design," we embark on a journey through the timeless wisdom embedded within these narratives, exploring their profound impact on modern psychology, healing practices, architecture, design, popular culture, science, and personal transformation.

Through fifteen captivating chapters, this book delves into the origins of myth, their psychological impact, and their therapeutic applications. It examines the influence of myth on design and architecture, the symbolism of mythological creatures, and the role of myth in shaping cultural identity. We explore the intersection of myth and technology, the future of myth, and the ways in which these ancient stories continue to inspire creativity and foster healing.

Whether you are a scholar, a designer, or simply a curious reader, "The Anatomy of Myth" offers valuable insights into the enduring relevance of these ancient narratives. By uncovering the timeless wisdom of myth, we can gain a deeper understanding of the human experience and harness the power of storytelling to inspire a better future.

www.ingramcontent.com/pod-product-compliance
Lightning Source LLC
LaVergne TN
LVHW010444070526
838199LV00066B/6194